# Healing Rainbows

# PEACE

# HEALING RAINBOWS

Embracing LGBTQIA+

Communities

with Scriptures

W. E. SMITH

Author: W.E. SMITH

Project manager W.E. SMITH

WillHouse Publishing LLC


This book may be purchased for educational, business, or sales promotional use. For information, kindly contact the author.

HealingRainbowsBook@gmail.com

WillHousePublishing.com

Unless otherwise noted, Scripture quotations are from the King James Version (KJV), 1604 or The American Standard Version (ASV), officially Revised Version, Standard American Edition, 1901

# WISDOM

# DEDICATION

This book is dedicated to all the victims of

misguided religious abuse and to all the people

that I have personally misled in my ignorance

over the years. I was absolutely wrong and I

sincerely apologize!

# GRACE

# ACKNOWLEDGEMENTS

I want to thank all those people who stood by me when many of those from the religious world attacked me. I appreciate all of you who texted me, called me, and privately messaged to encourage me to keep going, to keep telling the truth. Thank You for believing in me! Last but not least, to my readers, Thank You all.

Special Thanks to Kendra Malone, Freddie Turner, Desiree Alexandria, Chris Miller, Kayle Mack, Marcel Lee, Timia Dye, and Destiny Smith. You all in some way were a blessing as well as a guide to me in the completion of this book. I absolutely Appreciate You!!

# MERCY

A sincere apology in advance in case any language or terminology in regards to the LGBTQIA+ Communities comes across as offensive or degrading. I received counsel from members of the communities and I tried my best to be respectful. But there are ancient documents, bible verses, and quotes used to make points in this book that are concerning but needed to do the work of Healing and Understanding that this book promotes.

LOVE

This work of Love is
FOR the LGBTQIA+
Communities but
TO the Religious
Communities

# HEALING

# Table of Contents

# EMBRACING

# PREFACE

Long before I became an advocate for the LGBTQIA+ community I was one of its loudest opponents. I was guilty of using these very same verses of scripture to attack homosexuals for many years. I hope that this book will encourage and heal the LGBTQIA+ communities from the misguided interpretations of the bible that have been wounding the communities.

For those reading this book, who are not a part of the communities, Please be aware that this book is not written to force opinions, but to help you see truths for yourself, I ask you to think about and pray about the discussions and points that would be listed in this book. To use your common sense or if you believe in it, use the guide of the Holy Spirit to decide for yourself. On every controversial topic in this book, you will see a question that is meant to make you reflect or think about the topic and make the decision for yourself.

Religious people like me have been forcing our beliefs on people for years, this book is not about that. I am a church boy. I was raised in religion and with all the good things I learned, I also learned about religion's negativity, abuse, ignorance, and hypocrisy. I was taught to believe that homosexuality is a sin, an abomination, etc., and taught how they would burn in hell for all eternity. All of these were normal things to hear in church. Let me be clear in stating the fact that not every church did or does this but I am referring to churches like some of the churches I attended growing up. The earth is filled with loving, kind & compassionate Church folks, religious people, and Christians that have never turned their noses up to anyone, from any community. I applaud those wonderful human beings and wish I behaved as honorable and as Christ-like as they do but I wasn't taught that way growing up in church. This book is for people who grew up thinking like I did and this book is written from a place of love for both the LGBTQIA+ communities as well as the religious community. I was the main offender and this is my apology letter for my bad actions as well as other misguided church folks. John 8:32, "We shall know the truth and the truth will set us free!"

CHAPTER

1

# MYTHS AND LIES

In this little book we will discover the truth
about whether homosexuality is an
Abomination or not. We will expose the Myth of
God destroying Sodom and Gomorrah because
of homosexuality. We will look at the evidence
in scripture for homosexuals Being born Gay,

with a possible confirmation from Jesus Christ Himself and much more.

This book is designed to heal you, liberate you, bless you, and educate you.

Diverse opinions have been made about homosexuality for years, especially by the Christian community, it is regarded as sinful and an abomination, but is it? Does God really frown upon it or is it a narrative handed down by Religions or societal values to paint a certain picture about one's sexuality? Well, we're about to find out as we attempt to separate the truths from the myths.

While writing this book I had moments of doubt as to whether I was the right person to do this or not. Maybe this should be written by someone who has always been a member of the community or someone who has been fighting for LGBTQIA+ rights for decades but I've discovered that there appears to be a great divide between the Religious community and the LGBTQIA+ communities. It seems both sides view one another as extreme and irrational. Personally, living the extreme religious radical lifestyle for decades has given me a unique perspective into how religious people view the communities, as well as the best ways to communicate truth and disassemble myths that have been taught in error, in a way that extremely religious people can digest. With that said, I want members of the LGBTQIA+ communities to understand that the religious community is not always attacking due to prejudice or disdain but simply because of believing in things being taught to them as coming from the mouth of God. Many believe in their own as well as your salvation from Hell being tied to following those beliefs. Many religious people Love the communities and are simply trying to save you from burning in hell for eternity. But I believe we have learned some things that are incorrect and I will clear up every issue in this book. Now note that the points to be made are to expose biblical Myths and bring out facts from the Bible as well as some historical books and see their alternative points of view regarding this situation.

What exactly is a myth?

Definitions from Oxford Languages state that the definition of a Myth is,

> 1. A traditional story, especially one concerning the early history of a people or explaining some natural or social phenomenon, typically involves supernatural beings or events.
>
> 2. A widely held but false belief or idea.

This book is a result of a group of videos I did on my youtube channel, (Us Crazy Christians) where I debated and debunked every scripture used by the church to condemn or beat up the homosexual communities. With this book as was my heart in doing those videos, I simply want to give you information and allow you to decide the truth for yourself. I was extremely excited to release those videos believing that they could be the beginning of healing or relief for the LGBTQIA+ communities who have been abused or victimized by religious communities. But because I have been a church boy all my life, most of my acquaintances and the vast majority of my social media audience that I have access to are Church folks. My controversial videos only served to cause much conflict with my religious audience.

Although I did receive some private messages, DM's, and calls from people who were extremely blessed, encouraged, or set free by my videos, the majority of my DM's, calls, and texts were harsh criticisms and attacks. I was called, Satan, The Antichrist, a Heretic, a Faggot, and on my way to Hell to burn for eternity, etc. But even with all that meanness, I am proud to say that no one was able to prove me wrong! You may not like what I say and you may choose to disagree with my evidence but proving me incorrect will be extremely difficult. But I have decided to retire from debates and arguments. They never seem to produce positive fruits. So instead I have faith in You that you will view the evidence and decide for yourselves. My hope is that this book can reach the audience that my videos could not. For example, there are Christians like me who use the bible to attack the LGBTQIA+ communities simply because it is what we were taught in religion. We had no personal malice or hatred for the communities, we are simply misled to believe we are correct and are doing the will of God. There are homosexual Christians who love God but believe God hates them or disproves their communities. There are family members who have loved ones who are a part of the LGBTQIA+ communities and they are in turmoil being torn between accepting and supporting a loved one and what they believe the bible says about a loved one being tormented and burning in the flames of hell for all eternity. I want to reach all of these people with the Truth. That neither the bible, the scriptures, nor God Himself has any issue with you or your communities. I do realize that the LGBTQIA+ communities suffer attacks from other religions besides the Church but since I have spent nearly half a century in the Church and studying the bible, that is where I am best equipped to tackle this issue. I am also aware of the possibility that there are likely verses of scripture and biblical examples that confirm the LGBTQIA+ communities that I may have missed. I want this book to be an exhaustive reference book to aid in healing our collective communities. If you have discovered other confirmations or myths in scripture, maybe in other religious books, like the Book of Mormon, The Quran, The Tripitakas, etc. then please email me at HealingRainbowsBook@gmail.com and I may add your wisdom and revelations in a future revised edition.

After this book was written, I wanted to have it proofread by members of the LGBTQIA+ communities to make sure I wasn't being offensive or severely off with terminology for the communities, etc. It was shocking to me to realize how so many in the LGBTQIA+

communities disagree with one another on many things, just like how the White community or the African American Community don't all agree with each other in their individual communities. For a moment I felt overwhelmed with the task of trying to please or simply not offend anyone in the communities. Then I remembered my aim and purpose for this book. This book is written **TO** the Religious Communities **FOR** the LGBTQIA+ communities.

This book is for Pastors, Deacons, Youth Pastors, Ministers, Evangelists, and religious leaders of all religions and denominations and for Religious Parents who Love God and their

LGBTQIA+ children and are torn between their love for both. This book will heal and set them free to Love without condemnation. But I NEED THE HELP OF THE LGBTQIA+ COMMUNITIES to get this book into the hands of their religious friends and family members. It is very likely that if I attempt to go directly into churches or religious organizations with this information It will be immediately banned and blocked before the member of these churches or organizations even have a chance to read the book but If members of the communities can spread the book to family members, friends, share it on social media, etc., then this information can spread like wildfire, it can get past the religious gatekeepers. We can effect change in the religious communities forever. I'm excited about that!

Please read the brief Preface if you haven't already, just for a better context of this book and my motives. Let's get into it.

# STRENGHT

CHAPTER

# 2

# MY TRUTH

I am giving a PTSD trigger warning to members

of the LGBTQIA+ communities before you get

into this chapter. No question that many of my

attitudes and behaviors were wrong but I need

to be completely honest about my journey and

how I came to write this book For You. Also, I

am aware that being a member of the LGBTQIA+ Communities is not a Lifestyle or more than a lifestyle but because that is how many people especially members of the Church Community view the LGBTQIA+ Communities, I will use Lifestyle at times only to be clearly understood by using familiar language.

One day, when I was about the age of 13 or 14 my brother and I were walking to a corner store, and a man in a car drove right past us and slowed down, he blew a kiss to me and my brother. I immediately felt rage within me and started chasing the man down, hitting his car and throwing rocks at him. He just laughed and then he sped off. I turned to my brother and saw he wasn't as angry or moved as I was. I immediately grabbed him by the collar and threatened him to never let another man blow a kiss at him again. I realized many years later what I didn't know then, that my brother was very secure in his sexuality but I was insecure about mine. I'll come back to that.

I felt like as long as homosexuals didn't mess with me then I have no business messing with them, that was my viewpoint. But as soon as they hit on me, just like the gentleman with the kiss or anything similar to that just triggered me. It felt like the wrath of God was coming upon me if I didn't do anything, and I lived like that for years until about the age of seventeen. I had just left the gym and I was waiting at the bus stop on a Friday night. There was one other person there who was huge and had jerry curls, he was a black man. He stood right next to me, then all of a sudden, he asked "Do you like going to the movies?" There was a movie theater right across the street, and then I answered him and said I go to movies all the time. I even went further and told him I go to the movies at least once a week. Then he said, "I like to go but I don't like to go all by myself ". I didn't think much of that statement, then the next minute he asked if I liked to go out to eat. I answered him and said "Yeah, I go when I can. I like to go to different restaurants to eat" and I told him my favorites and stuff like that. Then he said "Me too, I just don't usually have anybody to go with" At that point, I kind of realized what was happening.

Once I became sure that the guy was hitting on me, anger immediately rose in me. I was filled with rage and my eyes felt like they turned red, I clenched my fist and turned to him, about to square up. But all of a sudden, I looked at him closely, and I immediately calmed down. This dude was twice my size and he was very muscular, so I wisely decided to take a deep breath and let it go. This guy offered me money, he tried to take me out and said he would buy me stuff, take me to dinner and give me this and that, he just kept on promising different things.

I turned him down repeatedly but that did not stop him, he kept telling me different things and promises but I politely turned him down because, at this point, I would normally be on the verge of fighting him, punching him, or being up in his face or something but this guy was so big and intimidating that he forced me to wisely choose the peaceful route. I was very irritated about the whole thing but I just kept saying " I'm fine, thank you, I'm not interested " and stuff like that but he didn't listen, he was still coming at me with different things, eventually pulling money out of his pocket to entice me but this honestly just made more irritated and bothered.

Luckily the bus finally came and we got on. The bus was crowded and there were people everywhere. The atmosphere was filled with different kinds of noise, talking, music, kids crying and laughing, and all other activities. I sat on the bus praying the big guy wouldn't come to sit next to me. The guy enters the bus but doesn't sit near me, he goes and sits behind the driver who pulls off, and all of a sudden the big guy lets out a scream and smashes both his fists into the seats and he puts his head back on the window. The bus driver immediately stops the bus, the noisy bus becomes quiet immediately, there was not a single sound made by anyone, and the whole bus went completely silent. Maybe about 15 to 20 seconds later the bus driver started driving again. Now that I think of it, I do not remember there being any noise on that bus until I got off of it. So as the drive continues, I hear a voice in my head say "That nasty faggot mad because you won't give him none of your booty." To some who aren't offended, this may sound funny now but I didn't find it funny back then.

I was so upset and was filled with so much anger at that moment. My mind flashed a vision before me and I saw what I was going to do. While his head was laid back against the

42

window and his eyes closed, I was going to walk up to him and kick him with all my might on his chin and knock his head through the window. If I was successful, I probably would have killed him. I was not being logical at all because I was full of anger. I got up out of my seat and was ready to walk up to this guy and as I reached the aisle out of my seat, I heard someone yell "Sit down!" aggressively. I turned and began looking around because I wanted to see who had just yelled at me and everyone was still completely silent. Nobody was even looking at me which made me freak out, I mean I just heard someone yell at me to sit down. I kept looking and waiting for a reaction but I got nothing, then

I'm thinking is someone pulling a fast one on me? Is this supposed to be a joke or something? I finally sit down, and after I do that I believe I heard God say to me "William, he was not hitting the seat and yelling out because you didn't give him your booty, he did that because he's a Christian just like you, he's one of my children and was upset that he gave in to his lust, and he was mad at himself for doing that. That was on a Friday, two days later on Sunday morning I went to visit another church, which was one of the biggest in the city of Detroit. I went there with some friends of mine and I saw that same brother with the jerry curls in the church walking past me and that did something to me. From that moment on I had a paradigm shift, it changed my view slightly about homosexuality and homosexuals in general.

I looked at them more as brothers in a struggle as opposed to looking at them like they were an abomination. I began to feel like I understood their struggle. I have that battle with ladies and trying to turn them down on my own and staying away from wanting or having sex with girls and getting mad about losing or giving in. I felt like God set me up because, in a normal situation like this, my anger would have gotten such a negative, possibly violent response, but he set me up in a situation with some guy that I couldn't imagine trying to fight.

So it made it to where I was able to learn something. He was able to teach me and help me see a different viewpoint than I previously held. It also taught me how my anger can blind me to logical or rational thinking. I felt ashamed.

I believe that God taught me something about myself in that there was some insecurity about my sexuality. The reason that I would be so angry and filled with rage when they hit on me or flirted with me was because of my insecurity or doubt about my own sexuality. I would play Jacks with the girls, jump ropes, and softball with the girls as opposed to playing baseball or basketball with the boys. I knew all the pattycake games as well as little Sally

Walker and all other girly stuff, and I wasn't the most masculine boy. After strong reflection and self-examination, I realized that I enjoyed Jax, hopscotch, softball, etc, not just because they were fun but because those are the games girls played and I wanted to play with the girls because I liked girls from a young age and loved being around them. Still do. But of course, a common question I get asked for my defense of the LGBTQIA+ family is, "Is William gay? Is he doing those videos & writing this book because he's gay?"

The answer is no. I just want to spread love, peace, joy, safety, and all of that. I have no hidden agenda, in-fact my only agenda is Love.

So for all of the Christians and even members of LGBTQIA+ communities who thought that the only reason someone would write this is that they're a member of the community is wrong because all of this is based on pure love.

I have been the victimizer; I've been the Christian bully and I want to rectify that. God has shown me that I was wrong and I want to fix that in the best way I possibly can and that is all.

So after the bus incident, and the paradigm shift I received, I was honestly still grossed out by the idea of homosexuality but I wasn't upset or angry by it anymore, I felt more kinship or understanding towards it.

A few years later I ended up having another paradigm shift, it was when the show I Will and Grace came out. It was my favorite show! I would laugh so hard at that show. One day my pastor was in the pulpit preaching and he went on a tirade about homosexuality and how they are trying to force their demonic homosexual lifestyle on us, especially thru tv, and at that moment, I was convicted because I felt like the homosexuals had tricked me. They had me laughing and joking about a show about gay people, they had deceived me! The devil was busy. I felt like the devil was using homosexuals by making them craftier than we the Church and it was my duty to stop them. At that moment I felt like God had chosen me to defend the Body of Christ against the attack from hordes of hell known as the Gay community. Now I was very good at debating against Jehovah's Witnesses, the Black Nation of Islam, Mormans, etc, not only would I be armed with all of the Bible studies that I'd do daily, I made it my job to learn about their writing and books so that I could use their writings and sayings against them and that was my plan against the homosexuals. I believed they were coming to destroy our way of life. Hell No! Not on my watch!

So I began to interview some homosexuals and appeared as a sympathetic ear towards understanding their plight but the real plan was that I was looking for ammo to use against them in equipping myself as a weapon to destroy the coming onslaught of homosexual hordes of hell. In my mind, there would be hell to pay, literally if something wasn't done to stop them, LOL. Sounds so silly as I write this but I promise I was as serious as a heart attack. I didn't play church then and I don't play church now! Souls and the Kingdom of God hung in the balance in my young, immature and religious mind.

During my interviews and conversations, I began to notice a reoccurring trend or theme of how so many of the people I talked to said they didn't want to be gay and that flew right in the face of me thinking they choose to do this. They would say stuff like "I don't want to be gay. I wish I wasn't born gay, I don't want to be attracted to men. I've had some of them come to me and say they hated the fact that they were gay and that they would constantly punish themselves every time they had a thought about another guy, none of this sounded like someone who chose to live that kind of lifestyle. To the church, I want to let it be known that not all people in the LGBTQIA+ communities have or have ever had these feelings but because Church was my life at that time I only had access to members of the community who were also Christians and had been bruised and beaten repeatedly with scripture telling them how accepting that lifestyle would lead to damnation, hell and displeasure from God. I then began to hear about the suicide attempts, feeling of abandonment, loneliness, and fear. I began to hear about all the abuse they suffered in school while growing up and how some of them would go to their Christian or Muslim parents some of whom were pastors, leaders, teachers, and deacons. etc., and how they would kick them out of the house even as young as twelve years old because he came to his parents to seek help because he was gay and had all these feelings he couldn't control and it shocked me it changed me, I began to have another paradigm shift in my thinking. Maybe I was wrong and had been wrong all along!

Consider this, one of the most pleasurable, loving things that we can experience in this lifetime is a loving committed relationship. It is strived for by the majority of the planet. But for the LGBTQIA+ Christian, it has to be the most despised and troubling idea, because for them to be a Christian they have to, in essence, refuse to ever receive that kind of love in a committed loving relationship, think about it. It has to be horrifying every time they hear someone talking about falling in love, and stuff like, he proposed to me and I said yes. Imagine you're a Christian who has to deny the feelings you have for someone you love because they are the same gender as you. It has to be the biggest tease ever to constantly see something flaunted in your face, but never be able to purchase it, you can never buy it, you can never have it.

This chapter is almost over. Please give me a moment to finish exposing my heart, then we will expose some myths.

A Christian gay man may feel that if he loves God and if he loves Jesus, they can't love another man. But if they do fall in love with another man, then they no longer love Jesus or God. And even worse, maybe because they do, they are no longer loved by Jesus Christ or God. These people are begging God to take that away from them, they are crying out to God embarrassed and confused, and they are wounded and hurt. They are crying to God and begging him to help and save them, to change them and fix them. They are brutally punishing themselves when they have a thought about someone of the same gender, fasting all the time, condemning themselves, and keeping their bodies under subjection. Refusing Love!

I remember there was one young man who was sitting in front of me with tears in his eyes, expressing to me how many years he had begged and cried to God to take that desire away from him. He didn't want it and he keeps rebuking the devil, going to deliverance services, crying out, praying, talking in tongues, and doing everything he can to make his desires go away, he's been begging God to help him. Yet God didn't. Maybe God had better things to do than to answer prayers and supplications, mingled with tears for years, maybe God's too busy to pay attention to that petty stuff. Or maybe God doesn't heal them or fix them because they were never broken in the first place.

Some of us preach and teach that God will destroy America as he did to Sodom and Gomorrah because of homosexuality, put yourself in their place just for a moment. Imagine you're a twelve-year-old boy sitting in church, imagine hearing your pastors saying that because of your feelings that you have for the same sex, that you don't want, that God is going to destroy you in hell for all Eternity, destroy your city and this country for other people that have the same desire as you that you don't even want to feel. Can you imagine what kind of pressure that is on some young Christian boy in church? Can you understand why the suicide rate is so high among young homosexual men? Can you see their pain? Can you feel their anguish? Even if it's just a little bit. What a burden to bear. A large portion of the church has said that for God to love them and allow them in heaven, they have to decide to live in hell on earth first. They have to choose to never live in peace and joy for their entire life on the earth. They have to pretend to be something they aren't. They have to pretend to love someone they don't, they have to pretend to be attracted to someone they aren't. While you are in love, calling your woman every day, dreaming about your man at night, walking in a park holding her hands, carrying her books or writing him poems e.t.c., the gay Christian twelve-year-old boy lives in constant fear of those same feelings.

Can you imagine living your entire life and never for once being in a loving relationship? How many of your friends, children, loved ones or parents died never knowing love, that you've probably experienced over and over again and you possibly even take for granted. They went to their graves probably never experiencing it, not even one time because of society, mainly the religious community. They lived in shame and secrecy. fear, loneliness, and lovelessness. Never knowing the kind of love that many of us in the straight community take for granted. Many of us have likely experienced relationships and falling in and out of love several times with several different boyfriends or girlfriends. While they went to the grave, they probably never even had one experience. Let that marinate.

I was in a relationship with a young lady and all during our relationship she constantly accused me of cheating & being unfaithful but honestly, that was the furthest thing from the truth. I was completely in love and loyal to her but I found out later in our relationship that she was the unfaithful one. Although I gave her no evidence or proof of infidelity, she was constantly pointing the finger at me in an attempt to keep my focus off of what she was doing and possibly even trying to ignore or filter her guilt. Is it possible that we as a church do the same thing to the LGBTQIA+ communities? We ignore our sin and to avoid feeling sad or guilty about it we enthusiastically point our finger at something we don't do or maybe we want to do

but are not free to do?  Let's expose some myths!

# 3

# SODOM AND GOMORRAH

There are a lot of opinions and criticisms in the church about homosexuality. In some churches, they are presumed evil, disgusting, weird, and an abomination before God, they are also discriminated against, harassed, and mishandled by some Pastors, Deacons,

Evangelists, Prophets, and church members. Is this right though? Is this Godliness? Is that the best way to deal with the situation? Could they be perfect just the way they are? One of the strongest weapons I used to hammer home how ungodly the homosexual community is was the biblical story of Sodom and Gomorrah and how God was so upset with the gay community that He completely destroyed that city by fire from the heavens turning it into ash!

But if you look closely, atrocities were committed in that city like rape or to be more specific, gang rape! The scripture gives an account of a large group of men about to brutally gang rape two men but I admit that my prejudice was so blinding that I just chose to focus on homosexuality as the cause of the fall of Sodom and Gomorrah. I'm not alone in this error of judgment. I can't help but think it Interesting that a lot of us Christians are convinced that the Cities were destroyed because of homosexuality when there are absolutely no verses of scripture that confirm that, not a one! There is clear scriptural evidence that explains an entirely different reason for its destruction. Is it possible that we chose to point that particular sin out and heap the blame on it simply because it's convenient? I also find it extremely disheartening that we can see clear biblical evidence for attempted gang rape and ignore it completely simply to focus on homosexuality. By this reaction and response to scripture are we Christians subconsciously claiming that the homosexual community is more horrible than a brutal gang rape?

A Homosexual relationship is two consenting adults of the same sex who have chosen to express their love for each other without bothering anybody, yet it is sadly still viewed as sinful, ungodly, or wrong. Some Christians would state the fact that Sodom is where the term "Sodomy" was coined, however, historians have said for decades that the origin of Sodom is based on assumptions of the scriptures and not the original definition.

The Bible does not say that Sodom and Gomorrah were destroyed because of homosexuality but gives the real reason for Sodom's destruction in Ezekiel 16:49-50 which says:

49. "Behold this was the iniquity of thy sister Sodom: pride,     the fullness of bread  and prosperous ease were in her and in her daughters; neither did she strengthen the hand of the poor and needy.

50. And they were Prideful and committed abomination before me: therefore I took them away as I saw good."

[American Standard Version]

In another version it reads.

49 "Behold, this was the iniquity of thy sister Sodom, pride, fulness of bread, and abundance of idleness was in her and in her daughters, neither did she strengthen the hand of the poor and needy.

50. And they were haughty, and committed abomination before me: therefore I took them away as I saw good." [King James Version]

Please allow me to mention that the abomination referred to in verse 50 is mentioned directly before it in verse 49, where it speaks of

Pride or haughtiness. According to scripture, Pride or Haughtiness is an abomination and hated by God. We will get more into that in the next chapter. Sodom was referred to twenty-eight times in the scripture, even Jerusalem is compared to Sodom and it is never referring to homosexuality but every time Sodom is compared to Jerusalem or any other person it is always talking about them being greedy, prideful, or not taking care of the poor, etc. So where then did we Christians get the narrative that Sodom and Gomorrah were destroyed because of homosexuality? Is it possible that we have allowed our prejudices or self-righteous judgments to blur our vision, hindering us from seeing the clear truth in scripture? Pray about it

and decide for yourself.

# 4

# ISN'T IT AN ABOMINATION?

Some religious leaders have debated me by stating that scripture says, Homosexuality is an abomination before God which is even worse than sin. Because an abomination means that God detests it with so much passion and disdain, alluding it is something that should never be committed. They are referencing a verse of scripture in Leviticus chapter 18, verse 22, which reads: "You shall not lie with a male as with a woman; it is an abomination."

My response is always that Proverbs 6:16 says:

16. There are six things which Jehovah hateth; Yea, seven which are an abomination unto him: [American Standard Version].

Let's go further and look at the other verses in the King James version and see what it says:

16 These six things doth the Lord hate: yea, seven are an abomination unto him:

17 A proud look, a lying tongue, and hands that shed innocent blood,

18 An heart that deviseth wicked imaginations, feet that be swift in running to mischief,

19 A false witness that speaketh lies, and he that soweth discord among brethren. [King James Version]

Now the abominations are listed from verse seventeen and they include Pride or haughty eyes, liars, murders e.t.c but interestingly homosexuality is not mentioned. But number one on that list is pride. Isn't it interesting that Proud people are not been chastised or treated like outcasts, this is number one out of all the abominations that scripture mentions God absolutely hates but we easily look around us and find out that a lot of us Christians are proud people and are walking about freely, not rebuked, no deliverance services scheduled to remove our pride. Why aren't proud people treated like an abomination as well? Some of us prideful people are even among those who insult and assault homosexuals, why is that? Is it possible that we Christians just picked whatever sin is easiest for us to condemn to take attention from the other sins we are committing? Aren't we being hypocrites by criticizing others when we are guilty of being abominable? The second abomination on God's

74

list references liars. I mean we've all lied before right? Maybe you never have, it's probably just me.

According to scripture lying is just as much a sin as homosexuality. I might argue that many verses clearly condemn lying as a sin and even an abomination but possibly not even one clear scripture condemning homosexuality as a sin. Interesting! So shouldn't liars be outcasts as well, I mean it's assumed that we all have lied many times in our lives regardless of how holy we claim to be, no one can likely claim they have never lied at one point or the other to save oneself or get ourselves out of some situations. Does that mean we're all an abomination unto

God? Let that marinate! I want to expose this hypocrisy that many of us religious people indulge in, by the way, hypocrisy is the sin most talked about from the mouth of Jesus Christ according to the Bible. Is it possible Jesus focused on that sin the most because we do it the most?

Again, I ask why aren't liars or proud people treated like homosexuals since according to scripture they are all abominations before God? As a matter of fact, a lot of pastors brag even in the pulpit. Some brag about their achievement, the number of souls they've won as well as how holy they are and how they hardly commit sin. Could that be the abomination of Pride? If a pastor exaggerates during his or her sermon or fudges the facts about his or her past, etc, is that the abomination of lying that God hates? God forbid a Christian lies to their child about Santa, the tooth fairy, etc. Ponder that.

Allow me to put in perspective that in the context of the Holy Bible, there are only about six to seven scriptures in the entire book that allude to homosexuality, but there are about fifty against lying, about 35 verses on pride, and a lot on hypocrisy, etc. Yet we don't see a lot of people being physically attacked or publicly embarrassed for being hypocrites or liars. How many of them are being rebuked, insulted, and ostracized? How many jobs refuse to hire proud people? Or, how many neighbors look at proud people with disgust and tell them to stay away from their children for just being a hypocrite or being proud? You definitely cannot compare that to homosexuals, who are being bullied and tormented every day in school, in their neighborhoods, at home, and even in the house of God. How many pastors stop in mid-sermon to point out and publicly embarrass the prideful couple in the congregation, calling them an abomination to God and declaring that they are going to hell? I have personally witnessed that happen to Christians struggling to abstain from the LGBTQIA+ lifestyle on many occasions in churches.

Again, I want to confirm that not all churches or religious people behave this way but this book is addressed to the churches or religious people who do. And not to condemn those who do because I know from first-hand experience that this is a belief passed down from generations and many are only trying to be obedient to God and what they believe God wants. This book attempts to offer new light on those views or beliefs of scripture. Lastly, have you ever witnessed a small child around seven or eight years old being stripped naked, teased, beat up, stomped & bullied on the playground just for being prideful or for lying! Absolutely not, but that has been happening to children born gay forever. Someone just froze reading the born gay statement because you are convinced that its a lifestyle choice but imagine if you were an eight, ten, thirteen or sixteen-year-old boy making that choice, would you abandon it after you realized the abuse you are destined to continue receiving every day for the rest of your life? Let that marinate for a moment and we will delve into the truth or myth of being born gay in the next chapter.

# 5

# JESUS SAID THEY WERE BORN THAT WAY?

In the Bible, Jesus spoke much about hypocrisy and pride but not one negative word about homosexuality. If God is bothered so much about it, then why didn't Jesus mention it like He did the sins like hypocrisy, pride, and lies?

I'm going to show you a verse of scripture where Jesus made an interesting statement. But first

Let me start by taking you on a brief but very interesting look through history.

In the ancient Middle East, under Assyrian law, homosexual acts were punished by castration causing them to become eunuchs. After I read that something clicked in my spirit and I began to do more research into Eunuchs. I found much more information than I plan to share in this chapter, so I encourage you to look further into some of the books I mention if you want more evidence. In the roman digest of laws, Lucien wrote about two ways to discover if a person is a Eunuch or not. The first is by checking their private parts to see if they have the proper equipment and the second is by their lack of ability to perform sexually with a female, if a female doesn't arouse him then he is considered a Eunuch. It's a historical fact that not all eunuchs are castrated, many were Eunuchs from birth according to ancient documents. In some ancient writings, the eunuch is said to be able to produce semen which is more confirmation that not all Eunuchs were castrated.

In the Talmud, Rabbi Eleazar asserts that Eunuchs by nature can be cured as opposed to man-made Eunuchs made so by castration.

Which is evidence that you can be considered a Eunuch without being castrated. You simply have to have no attraction for women. Sound familiar?

**{There is a point to all this and I will tie it all together in this chapter,**

**So please stick with me.}**

The Talmud said there are a lot of ways to discover if a man is a natural eunuch. Natural Eunuch means he was born that way and not a result of castration and not because he did not have male genitals.

Many ancient descriptions of Eunuchs described them as being feminine and not attracted to women and not castrated. I believe that the ancient term for homosexuality is 'Eunuch'. At this point you may be asking yourself, "What does this have to do with Jesus's possible confirmation of Lesbians, Gay, Transgendered, Bi-sexual, Queer, etc, being born that way as opposed to choosing that lifestyle". Let's go to the New Testament of the bible and read a quote from Jesus Christ, The Messiah, the Son of God.

In Matthew 19:12 Jesus says, "For there are eunuchs that are born from their mother's womb, and there are eunuchs that were made eunuchs by men: and there are eunuchs that made themselves eunuchs for the kingdom of heaven's sake. He that is able to receive it, let him receive it." [American Standard Version]

From the above Bible passage, it is safe to say that Jesus acknowledges the fact that

Some people were eunuchs from birth. In the world, at the time of Christ, it appears that Eunuch may have been synonymous with LGBTQIA+. Let's examine a few more historical documents and you can come to your own conclusion. In ancient classical literature, from the early fifth century BC onward, the word eunuch generally means the inability to or the abstaining from procreation whether due to a natural dislike of women or through physical mutilation. A late 19th-century article on

Chinese eunuchs called "Tong Shin" which means, "pure from birth" says, "Eunuchs were favored by the court ladies, they had no work assigned to them and they behaved like young girls." In "The Wisdom of the Sirach " one of the apocryphal books included in the Catholic Bible. It says, "That embracing a girl makes a Eunuch groan with nausea"! It also that, "A Eunuch has no more desire to have sex with a woman, then a righteous man desires to use violence." Again, notice how it states the lack of desire not the lack of ability. Aristotle wrote a warning that "If young boys continued to have anal sex they would become Eunuchs and not want to have sex with women." Aristotle also said, "Some would become Eunuchs from birth."

So it seems obvious from history and many historical documents that most people considered Eunuchs to be Gay men.

I am not attempting to justify or correct any ancient beliefs or viewpoints from these authors that I'm referencing, I am only trying to bring to your attention how they all seemed to view and describe Eunuchs in the same ways homosexual men are viewed and described today.

I could be wrong; I'm not trying to be right. I just wanna present some evidence and allow you to decide for yourself. It appears that the only definition the modern society held of eunuchs was being castrated but that was an extreme measure and wasn't even the norm for ancient Eunuchs. There are ancient writings talking about banning the eunuchs if they become attracted to women, why will that be an issue if a eunuch is castrated and can't have sex with Women? Which once again proves they weren't all castrated and could have sex with the women but if they did, they would be banned. Could this be referring to Bi-sexual Men? Let it marinate.

Alexander The Great is reported to have had a torrid love affair with his beautiful male eunuch. Using eunuchs as passive sex partners was a widespread custom across Mediterranean regions. The Jewish historian Josephus talked about a problem king Herod had with his eunuch companion with whom he was very fond of on account of his great beauty. Roman Emperor Hadrian erected statues of his beautiful male Eunuch lover Antinius throughout the Roman Empire and some of those statues still exist today. Several ancient documents state that a eunuch is unwilling and not unable but unwilling to have sex with a woman. This is very intriguing information. I can go on and on there are honestly too many ancient documents on Eunuch to address them all. If you want to learn more, I encourage you to research for yourself. What do you think? Is

90

it possible that Eunuch is the Ancient word for Gay or Homosexual? If eunuchs are homosexuals, then it is safe to say they are all over the Bible and many in very positive lights throughout scripture.

Let's just assume for a moment the possibility that Eunuch is an ancient term for Homosexual. Some examples of Eunuchs or powerful Gay men in the bible might be

1. Potiphar, the gay Egyptian official who bought Joseph as a slave

2. The killers of Jezebel

3. The court official Abimelech who saved Jeremiah the Prophet from the

dungeon

4.  The gay court officials of King Nebuchadnezzar who raised Daniel

5.  The gay servants who plotted against Queen Esther's father and the other gay servants who exposed the plot

6.  The gay court official called the Ethiopian Eunuch who Philip baptized

7.  Not to forget about the gay military leaders from Israel, Judah, Assyria, Babylonia, etc.

These people were all regarded as Eunuchs. Something to think about. Pray about it and decide for yourself. As I mentioned in the

Preface. This book was written from a group of videos I did on my youtube channel a few years ago. The information I'm sharing in this chapter started with two short videos on youtube by Pastor Jeff Miner titled "Jesus said some are born gay- Eunuchs part one and two. They are about 6 minutes long each. Then I found some blogs and articles online where people were debating this subject and they shared way more information about Eunuch than I do in this chapter I wholeheartedly wanted to share that site with you so you could read through the abundance of information they posted. But It no longer exists. I searched for a few days to no avail. One website that discussed it was www.whywouldwe.net but it no longer exists either. I could find several articles that talked about some of the things I mention in this chapter but none that shared as much or more information than I have already. But you can always do research for yourself in the books I've mentioned and you will see that I've only shared the tip of the iceberg on this subject of Eunuchs and homosexuality. Doing the research for this book I realized that Jeff Miner and John Connoley have co-authored a book titled The Children are Free: Reexamining the Biblical Evidence on Same-Sex Relationships. I'm not certain how much their book goes into Eunuchs but according to the online outline of the book

94

there is a chapter on the Ethiopian Eunuch and If his videos are any evidence then I'm sure they give more information than I do as I haven't even used all the evidence from his brief youtube videos. Happy hunting!

# FORGIVENESS

CHAPTER

# 6

# ISN'T IT IMMORAL?

Is homosexuality immoral? Now for something

to be immoral, you have to choose to do it, right?

If you are a straight man or woman reading this

book. Let me ask you if you choose to be

attracted to the opposite gender or were you just

born that way? Let's examine this for a moment.

Do we actually believe that a person will willingly choose to go through being alienated by family or all the horrible discrimination, humiliation, insults, pain, abuse, and sometimes even being beaten to death for having those desires? Who in the world would choose that lifestyle with those consequences attached? To straight men, can you choose to be attracted to another man? Right now, can you choose to have an erection by looking at another man? Absolutely Not! Unless you are Gay or Bi-Sexual.

Honestly, as I was writing this I decided to give it a try, I promise I did try to be attracted to men. I chose men I felt were attractive men yet I still could not imagine any romantic or sexual feelings without being completely turned off and that's me putting it lightly. I am a straight man and I was born this way, with this attraction, just as a gay friend of mine told me he couldn't even imagine being with a woman without getting sick to his stomach. They didn't choose it, it chose them. A closer examination of the scriptures being used to attack homosexuality, it appears that the scriptures, in almost every situation are tied to gang rape, temple idolatry, prostitution, or pederasty which was the practice of old men taking young boys as students and lovers. Could these things be what the scripture writers were condemning?

*Isn't It Immoral?*

You will be hard-pressed to find even one scriptural condemnation of a loving consensual relationship between two adults of the same sex. I could be wrong, look into it for yourselves if you care to.

CHAPTER

# 7

# ISN'T IT UNNATURAL?

Some of us church members will also say "But the Bible calls homosexuality unnatural". But unnatural means noncoital, meaning not involving heterosexual copulation. Driving cars, talking on a cellphone, flying in an airplane, etc is considered unnatural. Birth control is noncoital or unnatural, any sexual act that doesn't lead to the production of children is unnatural. The animal kingdom is a good example. Animals have been the gauge for what is considered natural for many years but animals engage in what's considered non-coaital or unnatural acts all the time. Animals have been known to kill each other, commit incest, and rape each other and it's considered natural, but does it make it right? Likewise looking at it closely, because something is unnatural doesn't make it wrong either.

For instance, the Israelites during biblical times as well as most ancient nations used the size of their tribe to equate power, and having a large number of children was considered a duty because they needed to grow their tribes in order to compete with tribes of other nations. Hmm....well this kind of seems like a logical reason why homosexuality or anything that prevented their clan from expanding would be viewed as an enemy and immoral since it would hinder their growth and power. Consider how in the Bible, Onah was killed for spilling his seed, and how a man refused to have sex with his late brother's wife and was killed for not giving her his seed. These examples show how any hindrance to growing their tribe was removed, but why isn't this talked about in church. Back then they needed to increase their population but that is not the case now, we have more than seven billion people on earth, and a lot of places are overpopulated, therefore not having a lot of children is accepted now, in fact, some countries even restrict the number of children a woman can have because of overpopulation.

Men do not go through fertility issues every month and can in fact give more children to the woman than she can handle, it's almost as if men were designed by God to be with multiple women, yet American society sees that as unnatural and immoral. Is it possible that anything can be unnatural to anyone by them simply being unfamiliar with it? Could it be

genuinely unnatural for a gay woman to be
sexually attracted to a man?

# COMPASSION

# 8

# HOMOSEXUALITY VS PEDOPHILIA

Some religious people have asked me if homosexuality is not a sin, does it mean being a pedophile is not a sin either? Well, there is a clear difference between these two scenarios and that difference is consent. The love between homosexuals who are of age is different from an adult who has sex with a child because a child is not old enough to decide whether he or she gives his or her consent to the intercourse or not. As a matter of fact, the Bible doesn't talk about Pedophiles, but we know it's wrong by common sense, right? If the Bible doesn't speak against it, then why do Christians? Please understand that I am vehemently against pedophilia but I'm simply trying to make a point. If the bible is the clear and concise rule book to be followed without restraint or question then by its clear ignoring of pedophilia ought we be doing the same? Absolutely not! But I do think that it's definitely a very interesting question.

In fact, most Scholars and Biblical Historians believe that Mary the mother of Jesus was about twelve or thirteen years old at most when she married Joseph. Yet we understand today that allowing a girl that young to get married is wrong based on American cultural norms and child psychology development theories as well as common sense and not the Bible. What about the scripture as well as the belief that God is the same yesterday today and forever. So if God was ok with young girls being married off to grown men as young as 12 in bible days, wouldn't He have the same opinion of that happening today? Think about it. The biblical characters were from a culture that didn't think sex with children was an offense. Maybe it was because it wasn't regarded as offensive or unnatural back then, isn't it possible that a lot of us Church folk are more followers of what a certain part of the scriptures says that benefits us than what Jesus says? Maybe we need to reconsider our thoughts on certain issues and look up to God for direction because it's very likely that there are some personal or religious biases clouding our view. This statement does not mean the Bible is bad, but it was written by humans and is therefore subject to the possibility of personal bias, after all not everything that happened back in time was in the Bible, and a body of scholars rejected some books which they considered unfit to be in the Bible.

The Holy Scriptures were voted on and placed in a book together over 358 years after the Crucifixion of Christ on the Cross. Did God put the bible together or did a group of religious leaders vote on it and disagree with one another with the majority winning the vote? History proves this fact! Scripture doesn't even call the bible the word of God; only the pulpits do that. Research it for yourself.

# UNDERSTANDING

# 9

# GOD SAID IT!

According to a lot of the Churches, the Bible
proves homosexuality is a sin before God, now
some Bible scholars beg to differ and argue that
these claims are a result of the Bible being
twisted by the writers of the scripture to suit
their own narrative. Of course, this is viewed as

false by many of us Christians as the Bible is believed as the voice of God. For many years I used to say that you can literally read some passages in the Bible and feel as if God is speaking to you directly even without praying so how is that possible if some narratives are twisted?

Lots of Religious people claim that they'll only follow what God says, and if He says it's a sin then so be it. But did God really say that? Look at things this way, have there been times you thought God spoke to you but you were possibly mistaken? Could it have been simply your own feelings, illusions, insecurities, or misinterpretations? For instance, a man wants to marry a beautiful woman, he wants to hear from God but has already determined in his mind that he wants to marry that beautiful woman, therefore he ignores the signs God gives and reorganizes or twists them to suit his narrative that she is the one for him. Or maybe his emotions for her are so strong that everything he hears or sees is filtered through his lens of desire for that Woman so it's easy to believe God is leading him to her. These kinds of things happen every day all over the world. Why do we believe the Bible writers were immune to their own desires, fears, beliefs, and insecurities? If a woman just sleeps and sees the Man she desires in the dream, she can see that as a sign that he is the one when it's just a dream. It is possible therefore that the bible writers in the past thought that homosexuality was a sin, just like Christians in the present think, and therefore wrote it off as a sin and simply added God's name to the verdict?

There is also a possibility that since they thought it was a sin, the writers through their own subconscious wrote it that way because they think they have heard from God. I mean our desires influence what we think we heard from God, this has definitely happened to everyone at one time or the other. Just like how Paul suggested that women cover their hair in the church to avoid distractions, some churches have taken it as the standard and even see it as a sin for women not to cover their hair during church services.

It is therefore possible that the writers of the Bible were influenced by trends, passed down beliefs and personal biases or possibly just wanted to force their biases because they thought it was right. If every word of the Bible is supposed to be followed to the core, then why are we Christians not selling our personal belongings and giving them to the poor, I mean according to the scripture this was clearly instructed by our personal Lord and Savior Jesus Christ, yet why isn't that followed in churches? And why are Christians who do not do that being discriminated against or abused? That's something to consider. We tend to believe that the Bible is the Word of God but the Bible calls Jesus the Word of God. The bible states that scripture is inspired by God and I can agree with that. The writer of the poem roses are red violets are blue was inspired by a beautiful woman but the beautiful woman didn't write the poem. Edgar Allan Poe said his tails were inspired by serial killers and murderers but not one of those killers or murderers wrote even a line of poetry for Poe, Poe wrote it. Comedian and Actor Kevin Hart said his comedy is inspired by his family but his family didn't write his jokes.

Is it possible that the Bible writers had God in mind, meaning they were inspired by God but God didn't touch one pen, nor did He instruct them in what to write? That might help to explain the many varying and disagreeing opinions about God throughout Scripture. Even Jesus corrected Old Testament scriptures as being incorrect but if God wrote it or instructed the writer in what to write then is Jesus correcting God? Let that marinate.

# SAFETY

CHAPTER

# 10

# RAPE SUPPORTED IN SCRIPTURE?

Maybe we should consider the idea that the bible isn't completely the best guide as to how to live our lives. Maybe the bible is not totally our best choice for a moral compass. Maybe it's simply a compilation of letters, songs, parables, and diverse opinions about God. If we choose to blindly accept the bible and all its writings as true, as God has written, or as the law then please allow me to present this verse of scripture for your consideration. Numbers chapter 31 says that God told Moses to go tell the Israelites to go kill all of the Midianite men, kill all the Midianite boys as well as all the Midianite women who were not virgins, and keep the virgins for themselves.

For a moment I want to ask you to imagine yourself as that young virgin girl, can you imagine any scenario of a girl wanting to marry or have sex with a man that killed her Father, her Mother, who murdered her brothers, her sisters, and her friends? Could you see yourself willfully marrying one of the Israelite men after that? Or could you imagine your daughter marrying your assassin after your assassination? These young women were taken forcefully during their overwhelming mourning and grieving period to be sex slaves to the Israelite men who brutally murdered their loved ones. With this in mind please allow me to add an additional layer of thought to this revelation of scripture. In the context of history, it is well documented that young virgin girls were being married as young as 12 years old which was absolutely normal in that region of the world and in that time period in history. So if the survivors of this slaughter were only the virgin girls they were likely female children under the age of 12 years old taken into captivity to be the concubines of Israelite men. Let that marinate.

This isn't Second W. E. Smith Chapter Two I'm referencing, these are our beloved Holy Scriptures. Scriptures many of us myself included for decades believed to be written by God or at least dictated by Him. Again I ask, Is it possible that the writers of the bible simply wrote what they believed and just attached the name of God to it, like men have done all throughout the history and the writings of every nation in the world, just as we do now? Maybe they were mere mortals just like us, with the

124

exact same prejudices, flaws, misunderstandings, and jaded opinions as we have now, maybe? Decide for yourself. Do you believe it's advisable to follow the Bible and do these same things just because it is written in there? Jesus told the Pharisees and the Scribes that they search the scriptures, for in them they think they find life, but they only point to me, yet you don't come to me. I think a lot of us in the church today are just like the Scribes and Pharisees, we claim to follow Christ Jesus, but the truth is we don't follow Jesus, we just say we do. We might be better to call ourselves Biblians as opposed to Christians but do we even follow the bible correctly? Better yet, should we?

This is a book in support of liberating the LGBTQIA+ communities through scripture and the only reason we have detoured into the subject of rape in the bible is to address the fanatical beliefs in the bible being flawless and free from men's opinions and biases. In the rest of this chapter, I want to give a little information about the definition of rape and some other possible examples in scripture. But I believe I've made my point with the first example so feel free to skip ahead to the next chapter if you want.

Rape is defined as unlawful sexual activity, most commonly involving sexual intercourse, carried out against the victim's will by force or threat of force, or with a person who is unable to give legal consent due to minor status, mental illness, mental deficiency, intoxication, unconsciousness, or deception. The crime of rape has been merged with the crime of sexual assault in several jurisdictions. Rape was often thought to be the result of unrestrained sexual desire, but it is today recognized as a pathological assertion of power over a victim. Since the late twentieth century, the legal definition of rape has evolved significantly.

Rape, according to the old meaning, was an act of sexual intercourse between a man and a woman against her will, regardless of gender or age. A rapist or victim might today be an adult of either gender or a youngster, according to the current understanding of rape. Although rape can happen in same-sex relationships, it is most commonly committed by a man against a woman. There is also a growing trend to consider forced prostitution and sexual slavery as kinds of rape when a husband engages in sexual intercourse with his wife against her choice. Rape, often known as sexual assault, can affect both men and women of all ages. The FBI defines rape as "the penetration, no matter how small, of the vaginal or anus with any body part or object, or oral penetration by another person's sex organ, without the victim's consent."

An attempted group rape is depicted in Genesis 19. When two angels arrive in Sodom, Lot welcomes them with open arms. The men of the city, on the other hand, gathered outside Lot's house and demanded that he hand up the two visitors to them so that they may rape them. As an alternative, Lot offers the mob his two virgin daughters. The crowd rejects Lot's offer, but the angels blind them, and God destroys the city, allowing Lot and his family to flee.

Also, Sachem had sex with Dinah in Genesis 34, however, how this text should be interpreted and understood is a point of contention among scholars. Many modern translations render it as 'raped' (or with the similar vocabulary of sexual forcing), whereas some previous critics recommended elopement. Another example is Tamar. Tamar's story resembles how most of us think about rape. There is little doubt that this is a rape story. The book describes Ammon's (her half-brother) cunning plot, the scene of deception, and Tamar's capture. Tamar begs and pleads for remedies to halt Ammon from rapping her, but to no avail, according to the author. She is then forced to live the rest of her life in shame due to social stigma. Everyone believes that this was a rape, even though the Hebrew text does not contain the word "rape" (there is no ancient Hebrew equivalent to our phrase). It is self-evident to us. First, Ammon wanted to have sex with his half-sister, which is considered aberrant in our culture. He ignores her pleas because she refuses.

Rape is a coerced and unwelcome act. It's not about sex; it's about power. To gain control over another person, a rapist utilizes actual force or violence — or the fear of it. Some rapists utilize medications to impair a victim's capacity to defend themselves. Rape is a crime, regardless of whether the perpetrator is a stranger, a date, a friend, or a family member.

# COMMUNICATION

# 11

# COMMON SENSE CHRISTIANITY

Even if the scriptures are clearly against homosexuality, does that in fact mean that God is? Isn't it possible that men put their own biases and opinions in their writings? This is definitely something to think, research, and pray about.

Something else I've noticed over the years. It appears that a good number of men and women who seemed to doubt their own sexuality or feel the need to reassure themselves that they are straight tend to be the ones who abused and ridiculed Gay people the most. Could that be a reflection of our own personal guilt? Maybe our guilt makes us fight harder and have the loudest voice against homosexuality?

It seems though that according to Interviews a lot of homosexuals' first gay experience was with the bully who teased, threatened, and beat them up the most. Now isn't that interesting! Might the abuse be because the bully had the same feelings, but was denying and fighting against them? There's a very important question I wanna ask, and that is "Who is the bride of Christ?" The answer according to scripture is the children of God, the church, us Christians. But aren't the children of God or the church made up of both males and females? Seems like Jesus didn't have a problem marrying both men and women, LOL. I was being a little silly with that question and the following comment but hopefully, you get the point.

The marginalized and outcasts were drawn to Christ and Christ was drawn to them. If we are followers of Christ and if our goal as Christians is to be like Christ then why are the marginalized and the outcasts not drawn to us? Instead, they hide from us, they fear us and if they are able to survive our abuse, they come back to defend themselves against us. We can debate the scriptures on homosexuality for many more years but I have to wonder if that's what Jesus would really want us to do.

Jesus commands us to love. God is Love & Jesus said they will know we are His by how we Love not by how often we attend service or read the bible and pray. 1 Corinthians chapter 13 says love is kind, love does not dishonor others, love keeps no record of wrongs, love always protects, and love never fails. These verses I just mentioned on love are a mere fraction of all the bible verses on love yet these few scriptures on love still outnumber all the assumed verses of scripture to condemn our LGBTQIA+ family.

Is it possible that the bible writers simply wrote under one of these two mindsets?

1. The writers were simply human and influenced by biases and taught beliefs just like we all are. Therefore, they heard God through the filter of their biases?

2. Some writers simply wanted to enforce their personal biases and knew that they would be more effective by simply attaching God's name to their own choices to give their actions more validity and acceptance?

Please pray about it, let it marinate, and use your own Sense of Christianity to decide for yourself!

# 12

# LET IT MARINATE

Let's say as a Christian you still don't believe in all these possibilities about homosexuality not being a sin, shouldn't we at least not discriminate against them or abuse them. Jesus Christ is love, and He taught us to love. In fact, He is the King of Love as He died on the cross for everybody, including those that hated Him. Scripture states that God is Love. Jesus commanded us to love our neighbor.

A lot of us Christians have caused the most scars, pain, and wounds to our LGBTQIA+ brothers and sisters. Jesus said, "they would know you are mine by how you love them". As a Christian, it is wrong not to love and pick at homosexuality which we may consider wrong as well as condemn the Gay community because were simply not Gay. Consider how some fathers are extremely overprotective of their daughters because they know what they do or did to other people's daughters, or how for instance a partner baselessly, without any evidence accuses the other partner of cheating at any slight incident because he/she actively indulges in cheating themselves.

Is it possible that people pick at other people's sins which they see as worse than theirs in order to cover their own sin or inadequacy or possibly to hide the fact they have those same desires? Their situation can be likened to how some abusive fathers speak. Imagine a man who abuses his wife or children telling them that they were lucky, they didn't get beaten up the way he was by his own father. That's exactly how it is, trying to shift the blame to his father to avoid seeing his own wickedness because his father was way worse. We have to ask ourselves this

"Are we as Christians trying to do these same things to homosexuals? Again, I'm not trying to convert or convince you of anything, believe whatever you want. This book is to offer alternatives if your current beliefs are causing you or your loved ones pain. So just for a moment let's all agree that Homosexuality is absolutely wrong. So what if it is! We are created and wonderfully designed to Love.

We are the happiest when we love and are being loved. It's unnatural to not love. Is it possible that if they are living in sin, that love is the only real solution? Jesus Christ dined with the so-called sinners, and they sat with him without fear. Why then do homosexuals feel fear of discrimination and being ostracized when they sit with us Christians who are by definition supposed to be Christ-like. Jesus himself drew them closer to himself, protected them, cared for them, and Loved them. Jesus is love, and love is beautiful, it is kind and compassionate. How would Jesus embrace the LGBTQIA+ communities? Ask yourself, "What would Jesus Do"!

# JOY

CHAPTER

# 13

# TRANSGENDER?

For many years I argued and debated against homosexuality, then I argued and debated in favor of homosexuality for years so I felt like I had some knowledge on the subject, even though there is no doubt that I have much more to learn but with that said. I honestly know very little in regards to scripturally defending Transexuals although I do support them based on the same information I've previously pointed out in this book.

So for this chapter, I found an amazing article from the Human Rights Campaign Foundation and Authors, Austen Hartke, Myles Markham, and Lead Editor Michael Vazquez. That article truly blessed me and I want to share a little of that with you in this chapter. If you want a more detailed and expanded understanding of the Trans community I strongly recommend going to the Human Rights Campaign and reading that wonderful article. My brief ep certs won't do it justice. In

Genesis, we find two stories about how things came to be, one of which says "So God created humankind in his image, in the image of God he created them; male and female he created them" (Genesis 1:27, NRSV). God creates men and women in Genesis 1, it's after creating opposites in every other corner of creation--day and night, land and sea, flying birds and swimming fish. Humans, then, are also created in an opposite pair--male and female. But the problem with a literal reading of this text is that even though Genesis 1 sets up these binaries, God's creation exists in spectrums.

In between day and night, we have dawn and dusk; between land and sea we have coral reefs and estuaries and beaches; between flying birds and swimming fish we have penguins and high jumping dolphins, not to mention that uncategorizable favorite the platypus! No one would argue that a penguin is an abomination for not fitting the categories of Genesis 1, or that an estuary isn't pleasing to God because it's neither land nor sea. In the same way, God gives every human a self that is unique and may not always fit neatly into a box or binary. Genesis 2 gives us a different perspective on the creation story, and here a non-gendered human is created first, and then later a piece of the first person, Adam, is made into the second person, Eve.

Deuteronomy 22:5, "A woman shall not wear a man's apparel, nor shall a man put on a woman's garment; for whoever does such things is abhorrent to the LORD your God," (NRSV) is the only verse in all of Scripture that directly references gender-based notions of clothing. While in many cases transgender people are not in fact "cross-dressing" (a term that implies one is *crossing* their gender identity rather than *confirming* it), but instead are affirming and reflecting their gender identity through the clothes they wear. Some are convinced that forbidding the Hebrew people from dressing in clothes associated with a gender different than their own was a way to be set apart from the Canaanite and Syrian religions where this phenomenon was a part of certain worship rituals. Other scholars believe the prohibition was more of a way to reinforce previous instructions from the Torah that forbid "mixing" (for example, not blending fabrics, planting variations of seed, or eating shellfish)

We are invited to pause, breathe and simply observe the work God is already doing. The experiences of gender diversity can be found in nearly every culture throughout recorded human history. Traditionally gender non-conforming people were given communal roles as spiritual leaders, healers, conflict mediators, and cultural conduits.

While not all of these experiences map perfectly onto contemporary trans experiences, what we do see similarly today are countless examples of transgender and non-binary people across denominations operating in specialized roles within the church whether formally recognized or not. Transgender and non-binary people are actively preaching, teaching, leading, pastoring, and offering their time, energy, and various gifts for ministry and service. What this tells us is that the real issue here is not whether a person can be transgender and Christian, but whether the church will acknowledge and empower those whom God is already working through to enrich the whole life of the body of

Christ. As we all approach this topic with compassion, humility, and courage, we may call to mind the words of Gamaliel, a teacher who defended the persecuted apostles of the early church: "...[I]f this plan or this undertaking is of human origin, it will fail; but if it is of God, you will not be able to overthrow them — in that case, you may even be found fighting against God!" (Acts 5:34-39, NRSV).

Again, please go read the entire article for yourselves. It is amazing, they even have scriptural and historical evidence to suggest that Eunuch may have been considered Transexuals. Among other great points.

In GLAAD's (Gay and Lesbian Alliance Against Defamation) media reference guide, under the heading "Terms to Avoid": "Do not say, 'Tony is a transgender,' or 'The parade included many transgenders.' Instead say, 'Tony is a transgender man,' or 'The parade included many transgender people.'" For example, if you meet a trans person—someone who identifies with a gender other than the sex they were assigned at birth—it's generally a good idea to ask which pronouns (he or she, him or her) they prefer and to use whatever that is. If you meet a trans person, you should not ask about the particulars of their body, much as you would likely prefer strangers not to inquire about yours. And if you meet a transgender person, you should not refer to them as "a transgender" or "transgendered."

In 2014 Time Magazine did an article on Trans people saying, Another misconception is that the defining part of being transgender is having surgery as if a trans person isn't *really* trans until they've gone under the knife and come out the other side fully "transgendered." "There's a tendency in American culture for entertainment and news outlets to focus on surgery, surgery, surgery," Mara Keisling, executive director of the National Center for Transgender Equality, told TIME in a previous interview. But, she says, while surgery is very important for some trans people, others have no desire to have surgery; they might not have surgery for medical reasons, religious beliefs, financial constraints, and so on. There's an "authenticity issue that trans people face," says Elizabeth Reis, a professor of women's and gender studies at the University of Oregon. "People are so focused on whether or not they've had surgery, as if that's the pinnacle of authenticity. Even if they haven't had it or if they haven't had it *yet* or they're never planning on having it, they still have these feelings about their gender." Avoiding the *ed* isn't going to solve that authenticity issue, but it doesn't hurt.

However, Keisling also says that focusing on whether the "ed" is tacked on the end of *transgender* can be a distraction. She believes it's more important for everyone to be having a conversation about LGBT civil rights issues than to wag fingers at people over terminology. "I don't ever want to say that communities or cultures can't have language variations," she says. "Language is very important and what people want to be called is very important. But we have to have a common language that we can bring people into. We have to have a language that they can grasp." And, she says, just as *transgendered* has become unpalatable, there's no telling what will be preferred down the line. Still, "for now," Keisling says, "I would use the word, *transgender*. Particularly if you are outside of the family, that's going to be okay." (If you have more questions about terminology, the GLAAD media guide is a great place to start.)

BLISS

# 14

# THE GAY AGENDA

Jesus said, in Matthew chapter 11 "Come to me and I will give you rest". Can the LGBTQIA+ person find rest or peace in your home or in your church? Or because of their sexuality, will they be singled and called out in the church or your home and referred to as dirty, filthy sinners and a candidate for the Lake of Fire? The church is supposed to be a safe space for the weak and defenseless, we are supposed to wipe your tears irrespective of whom you are and welcome you with love just as Jesus did, but we recognize that one of the biggest critics of the LGBTQIA+ communities is the church, we are among those that pushed them out or spat on them and referred to them as evil.

This means they have nowhere to turn to and they have to depend on themselves and each other or get consumed and destroyed. Yet the destroyers are we the Church who are supposed to be an example of love on earth, just like Jesus set an example of love. A lot of Christians will argue that they, though they don't treat proud people, liars or hypocrites, etc, like outcasts it's only because those sinners didn't shove the fact that they do these wrong things in people's faces, and neither do they try to force their own Agendas or narratives about their prideful or lying lifestyle or beliefs down people's throats like the LBGTQ+ communities does. In response to my arguments, I've been told that "Proud people and liars don't picket & petition the schools, churches, and courts to accept their prideful or lying lifestyles as normal". "They not trying to force themselves on us as the homosexuals do". But think about this. Isn't it a normal human instinct or reaction to cry out if you are neglected or being discriminated against? Don't babies and children cry when we ignore them? Don't we whine and throw tantrums if our lover ignores us? Don't you always try to prove yourself when people doubt you or try to bring you down constantly? But then again, a lot of us Church folks think if they weren't always in our faces or so flamboyant, then maybe the church would be more lenient towards them. If we look at it more closely though, it's human nature to react that way.

For example, African Americans were in slavery for hundreds of years, unable to wear nice clothes, not able to drive nice cars, and adult man and woman had to ask permission to do anything even as simple as going to the bathroom. So when we have an opportunity to do all those things we previously couldn't we can be flashy, as well as dogmatic about our freedoms, etc. We protest with one voice against discrimination and abuse, that's exactly how it is. African Americans are always in their faces, protesting, demanding equality and fair treatment, for decades that was considered as trying to force the black agenda on the world and many still feel that way today. Imagine how it feels when nothing is done about it, when no one comes to your aid, when no one wants to hear about your suffering, how we hold our heads in sorrow and go back home because there is no significant change. We awake to see that another black man was shot or abused. It is a terrifying feeling to realize that the hurt you feel or that the tears you cry are not heard, so yeah maybe being dogmatic about your mistreatment is a normal reaction? Have we ever thought maybe that's how homosexuals feel? It's likely that every African American has at one time or the other felt fear and pain from police brutality and harassment, to be hated for simply being born the way you are, just because you're slightly different from them. Is it anybody's fault they are black? Do they choose to be? Didn't we all just come out of our mother's womb and find out we are how we are.

As a black person, if you have experienced the pain of crying and not being heard for something you have no control over, then black Christians should at least understand, even if it's just a little, how painful and depressing discrimination can be.

Is it possible that if slavery and jim crow are responsible for the African American's response, then maybe the church is responsible for the LGBTQIA+ community's response? Maybe the church is complaining about the problem they created, LOL. Women know how it feels when men are made superior over them or treat them less than they deserve, how men are given certain jobs because society feels they would handle it better. Why do they cry out and stand up for themselves, forcing their agenda on society? The argument I get after making this point is that an African American or a Woman is born that way but a Homosexual chooses that lifestyle. Is it possible that Jesus and the Bible state that they were born that way? Hopefully, we have examined that idea strongly enough in chapter four.

# 15

# WHAT IS LGBTQIA+

**LGBTQIA+** is an acronym that stands for

Lesbian, Gay, Bi- sexual, transgender, and

Queer, or questioning one's sexuality.

**LGBTQIA** – Lesbian, Gay, Bisexual, Transgender, Intersex, Queer and/or Questioning, and Asexual and/or Ally

**Queer** – Queer is often used as an umbrella term referring to anyone who is not straight and not cisgender. Cisgender people are people whose gender identity and expression match the sex they were assigned at birth. Historically the term queer was used as a slur against LGBTQIA people, but in recent years it has been reclaimed by LGBTQIA communities. However, some LGBTQIA people still find the term offensive. Queer is also often used as a broad rejection of labels. In this context, this could be a rejection of any type of label, but most often refers to a rejection of labels for gender and sexual orientation.

**Questioning** – This term refers to someone who is not sure how they identify. Someone can be questioning their sexual orientation and/or their gender identity.

**Intersex** – This term refers to people who naturally have biological traits, such as hormonal levels or genitalia, that do not match what is typically identified as male or female. There are many different intersex variations. Being intersex is a naturally occurring trait in humans; it is not pathological. Being intersex is not linked to sexual orientation or gender identity; intersex people can have different sexual orientations and gender identities and expressions.

**Asexual** – Often referred to as "Ace", this is an umbrella term used for individuals who do not experience, or experience a low level, of sexual desire. This identity can include those who are interested in having romantic relationships and those who are not. People of different sexual orientations and gender identities can be asexual.

**Ally** – People who identify as cisgender and straight, and believe in social and legal equality for LGBTIQ+ people are allies.

**LGBTIQAPD** – Lesbian, Gay, Bisexual, Transgender, Queer and/or Questioning, Intersex, Asexual and/or Ally, Pansexual, and Demi-sexual.

**Demisexual** – Often referred to as "Demi", this is a term used to describe someone who can only experience sexual attraction after an emotional bond has been formed. This bond does not have to be romantic in nature

**Pansexual** – Often referred to as "Pan", this is a term used to describe a person who is sexually, romantically, and/or emotionally attracted to people regardless of their sex or gender identity.

**LGBTIQA+/LGBTQ+** – Adding a "+" to the acronym is an acknowledgment that there are non-cisgender and non-straight identities that are not included in the acronym. This is a shorthand or umbrella term for all people who have a non-normative gender identity or sexual orientation.

**LGBTIQ** – Out Right Action International uses the acronym LGBTIQ to denote the lesbian, gay, bisexual, transgender, intersex, and queer community. This acronym is inclusive of a broad range of people however, it is not exhaustive, nor is it universally accepted or used.

**Trans\*** – The asterisk next to trans refers to all of the identities within the gender identity spectrum, other than people who identify with the gender that they were assigned at birth. Including the asterisk after trans denotes a special effort to include all non-binary, genderqueer, and gender non-conforming identities.

**Non-binary & Genderqueer** – These terms are actively debated within the LGBTIQ+

communities. Both terms are similar in scope. Non-binary refers to people whose gender identity falls outside of the gender binary (i.e. either male/man or female/woman) and was coined as a descriptive term, used to describe experiences that fall outside of the binary gender model which undergirds much of society. Genderqueer refers to people who have a non-normative or queer gender. Genderqueer is often used to refer to people who reject labels and conformity to specific gender norms. Non-binary tends to be more of an umbrella term, which encompasses genderqueer people, along with other non-binary genders.

Their flag is represented by six colors of the rainbow. Homosexuality is not something new as it goes way back to the time of Christ and even before then and we can see that through some references in the bible. Homosexuality is when two persons of the same sex are attracted to one other.

The term comes from the Greek word homos, which means "the same. "Same-sex attraction can be experienced in a variety of ways. In their teenage years, many LGBTQIA+ plus persons develop affection for others of the same sex. It may take some time to figure out what you're most drawn to or to feel comfortable admitting it to yourself and others.

At different times in their lives, people have different sexual, romantic, and emotional feelings toward another person.

Homosexual behavior has been permitted, tolerated, punished, and outlawed at various eras and in diverse societies. Homosexuality was widespread in ancient Greece and Rome, and in recent years, Western classicists have focused on the connections between adult and teenage boys in particular. Homosexual behavior is considered wicked in both Judeo-Christian and Muslim cultures. Many Jewish and Christian leaders, on the other hand, have gone to great efforts to emphasize that their faiths forbid behaviors, not individuals or even their "inclination" or "orientation." A very popular phrase many churches use and I have used often myself in regards to the Gay community was, "God loves the sinner but hates the sin". Does He really hate that sin? Stick around and look deeper into it with me.

# TRANQUILITY

# 16

# HOMOSEXUALITY AND SCIENCE

The historical shift in the professional and scientific mental health community's attitudes on homosexuality is exemplified. Prior to 1975, homosexuality was regarded as a mental illness. Since then, however, the general view has been that homosexuality, as well as the entire range of sexual orientations, is a normal human variation with a biological origin. Alfred Kinsey, Ph.D., was one of the early pioneers of sexual study, and he is often recognized for advancing this historical transformation. He is regarded as a pivotal person in the history of sexual science, owing to his contributions a more comprehensive knowledge of sexual orientation. Sexual orientation is defined as the combination of sexual feelings, desire, arousal, fantasy, and attraction. Dr. Kinsey's most significant contribution to sexual science was the 17,000 interviews he conducted with Americans about their sexual life. Some have challenged Dr. Kinsey's study for relying on volunteers, resulting in a skewed sample. This is because people who choose to participate in sex research are more likely to be sexually active.

In the past, homosexuality was usually referred to as a mental disorder but this changed with time. Despite the fact that the American Psychological Association no longer considers homosexuality to be a mental condition, some mental health practitioners from many disciplines continue to treat homosexuality as a "fixable" disorder. Clearly attempting to change or reverse anything implies that it is undesirable and unhealthy (Murphy, 1992). Some of these doctors explain their treatments by citing their own religious beliefs, which hold homosexuality to be a sin.

CHAPTER

# 17

# FINAL THOUGHTS

I realize that this book deals with the Gays and
Lesbians more so than other letters in the
Rainbow but that Is primarily because the
scriptures and biblical myths are mostly geared
to those specific communities. But I believe that
if we can expose those misunderstood scriptures

then the truth and freedom will spread to all the LGBTQIA+ Communities.

Let's assume that the church is right and homosexuality is a sin, we cannot send them to heaven nor can we send them to hell, we cannot change nor fix them. Honestly, the church has tried unsuccessfully for centuries. So that means that only God can help or save them. So maybe we should just love them and draw them closer to the only one capable of fixing their problems instead of chasing them away. Some churches, "Thank God", have calmed down and are no longer running Gay and Lesbian people off, but they still look at them as church projects and people that need to be delivered and have the gay demons cast out, people that need curing, fixing, healing and so on. But that is not a place of peace, love, joy, or safety.

God's love is unconditional, because we are followers of Christ we should attempt to love like Jesus? If adulterers are allowed to feel safe in church, then why not homosexuals. If wife beaters, fornicators, liars, proud people, and the likes are allowed to feel safe in church then why not the homosexuals? Even if you leave this book in stark disagreement with me, can we at least agree to love? Can we at least agree to care for our gay brothers and sisters and not try to change them, because we can't? You may disagree with all the points in this book, but can you agree to love them like Jesus and trust in God to change them? And if he doesn't change them, can we still love them just as they are, unconditionally? And to our brothers and sisters in the LGBTQIA+ communities, **I Sincerely Apologize** because we've hurt, we've betrayed you! Not in malice but out of religious ignorance.

Please let me also reiterate that many people who have opposed you and still do, do it from a place of ignorance, misunderstanding, fear, and erroneous teachings. It is not always personal but simply misinformation. God made you perfect just as you are and He loves you Unconditionally! God doesn't love you in spite of who you are, He loves you because of who you are! When you have time please read Romans 14: 13-14, and Romans 8: 31-39.

I pray this book helps more people see and understand the truth and I hope and pray that this book can help to soothe some of the wounds we have inflicted upon you, mentally, spiritually, emotionally, and physically. **I Love, Value, Adore and Appreciate you!**